Northamptonshire County Council
Libraries and Information Service

ROADE

2 6 AUG 2004
3 SEP 2004
0 7 JAN 2005
2 4 FEB 2005
11 APR 05

Northamptonshire
DISCARDED
Libraries

BD	DV	BB	BR 02/03
DM	DX	BM	BV

My mum's put me on the transfer list :
football poems ; chosen by John Foster

Please return or renew this item by the last date shown.
You may renew items (unless they have been requested
by another customer) by telephoning, writing to or calling
in at any library.   100% recycled paper   *BKS 1 (5/95)*

OXFORD

UNIVERSITY PRESS

Great Clarendon Street, Oxford OX2 6DP

Oxford University Press is a department of the University of Oxford.
It furthers the University's objective of excellence in research, scholarship,
and education by publishing worldwide in

Oxford New York

Auckland Bangkok Buenos Aires
Cape Town Chennai Dar es Salaam Delhi Hong Kong Istanbul
Karachi Kolkata Kuala Lumpur Madrid Melbourne Mexico City Mumbai
Nairobi São Paulo Shanghai Taipei Tokyo Toronto

Oxford is a registered trade mark of Oxford University Press
in the UK and in certain other countries

This selection and arrangement copyright © John Foster 2002

The moral rights of the author have been asserted

Database right Oxford University Press (maker)

First published 2002

All rights reserved. No part of this publication may be reproduced,
stored in a retrieval system, or transmitted, in any form or by any means,
without the prior permission in writing of Oxford University Press.
Within the UK, exceptions are allowed in respect of any fair dealing for the
purpose of research or private study, or criticism or review, as permitted
under the Copyright, Designs and Patents Act, 1988, or in the case of
reprographic reproduction in accordance with the terms of the licences
issued by the Copyright Licensing Agency. Enquiries concerning
reproduction outside these terms and in other countries should be
sent to the Rights Department, Oxford University Press,
at the address above.

This book is sold subject to the condition that it shall not, by way
of trade or otherwise, be lent, re-sold, hired out or otherwise circulated
without the publisher's prior consent in any form of binding or cover
other than that in which it is published and without a similar condition
including this condition being imposed on the subsequent purchaser.

British Library Cataloguing in Publication Data available

ISBN 0-19-276295-8

1 3 5 7 9 10 8 6 4 2

Typeset by Mary Tudge (Typesetting Services)

Printed by Cox & Wyman Ltd, Reading, Berkshire

My Mum's Put Me on the Transfer List

Football poems collected by John Foster

OXFORD
UNIVERSITY PRESS

Contents

Northamptonshire Libraries & Information Service

Peters	12-Dec-02
C821	£4.99

Footballitis

I have football with my cornflakes,
I spread football on my toast,
I eat and breathe and sleep it,
It's the thing I dream of most.

Football posters in my bedroom,
Football stickers in my books,
My hair is striped in red and white,
I love the way it looks.

I watch television football,
I play football in the park,
I imagine winning matches
In the sunshine, in the dark.

I write football poems and stories,
I count footballs in my maths,
I score goals into dustbins
I dribble Coke cans down the paths.

I have football with my cornflakes,
I spread football on my toast,
I eat and breathe and sleep it,
It's the thing I dream of most.

Daphne Kitching

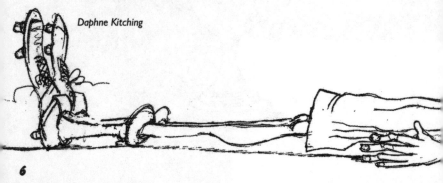

Football Fever

I've caught football fever
Now I'm football mad
Football's taken over
I've got football bad

Yes, I've got football fever
I thought I was immune
But I'm not *sick as a parrot*
Instead I'm *over the moon*

So I don't need a doctor
I don't need a pill
I'm not feeling awful
I'm not really ill

I've just got football fever
I've just gone football mad
I'm as crazy as my sister
As barmy as my dad

We've all got football fever
Each one did succumb
But if you think *we've* got it bad
Wait till you meet Mum!

Bernard Young

Football on the Brain

In the yard at ten to nine.
In the yard at break.
On the field at dinner-time
until our legs all ache.

Out there when it's cold and hard.
Out there in the rain.
That's the way with our lot:
Football on the brain.

Some like playing marbles.
Some like games of chase.
Some just like to muck about
and stand around the place.

But our lot run together
with passes swift and neat.
Our lot's always on the move,
a football at our feet.

Some say, 'I'd get tired.'
Some say, 'I'd get bored.'
But they don't know the buzz you get
when you're the one that's scored.

Some say, 'Why the trouble?'
Some say, 'What's the fuss?'
But our lot's off to Wembley.
That's the place for us.

Out there when it's cold and hard.
Out there in the rain.
That's the way with our lot:
Football on the brain.

Tony Mitton

Kicking In

I'm kicking my ball
against the wall
against the wall and back.

I'm practising how
to pass the ball
by kicking the ball
against the wall
against the wall and back.

I'm practising how
to launch an attack
by passing the ball
against the wall
and running to get it back.

I'm dribbling the ball
towards the wall
around the dustbin and back.

I'm beating defenders
one and all
as I dribble the ball
towards the wall
around the dustbin and back.

I imagine the goalie
coming out.
I hear the fans
all cheer and shout.
I shoot the ball
towards the wall.
He dives too late
it's through the gate!
And I've scored! I've scored!
I've scored!

John Foster

Please, Mr Black

Mr Black, Mr Black,
Please can we have our football back?
You can pass it through the window.
It'll fit through the crack.
Oh, don't be a spoilsport, Mr Black.
Please give us our football back.

John Foster

Live Football From Pete Symmonds's Garden

Good afternoon, sports fans, and welcome to
Live Football From the Back of Pete Symmonds's Garden
(*Or LFFTBOPSG for short*)
here in sunny Rochdale!

After twelve minutes of frenzied football
briefly interrupted by a can of Coke and a Mars bar
neither team (each comprising one brother)
has been able to score a goal
and so we find ourselves in a penalty shoot out situation!

And as I stride up to take the first shot
I hear Mum shouting to us to come in for tea:
I ignore and I shoot and I score!

And now it's young Paul Symmonds's turn
to come and take a penalty.
Mum shouts again.
He ignores, shoots, misses and . . .

OH NO, SMASHES A PANE OF GLASS IN DAD'S GREEN-
HOUSE!

And here comes Dad, red-faced,
striding over, not too pleased,
and he's taking out his cards
and the young lad Paul Symmonds is . . .
SENT IN!

And now Dad's looking at me,
I explain I had nothing to do with it
but he's SENDING ME IN AS WELL!

A harsh decision, I protest,
but the big man's not going to change his mind.
A quite remarkable finish to a memorable game.
Join us next week when Paul and I
will be playing football in the attic,
and hopefully we won't break anything.

Goodbye for now!

Ian Bland

Backyard Kickin

Kickin mi football gainst di wall
mi neighbours complain
but I no harm at all
kickin mi football
dat's all!

Kickin mi football out on di street
me and mi posse we compete
mi neighbours complain
but our answer is sweet
We kickin a football
dat's all!

Dad kick mi football at di weekend
Kickin so hard he pretend
he really de boss o' England!
Mi neighbours complain
they gotta window to mend
cos Dad kick mi football
over di wall.

Dat's all.

Chris Riley

Wiz

My pal's a wizard at footie,
the ball is under his spell:
when he dribbles it runs at his feet like a dog,
when he shoots it's a homing missile.

He flies down the pitch without effort
and seems always to know where to be:
it's much more than skill and practice—
it's soccer sorcery.

I'm sure he could play a whole team on his own
but that's not all there is to football—
he may be pure magic to watch
but he's no fun to play with at all.

Dave Calder

My New Football

Kick it, head it, dribble it.
Shoot it in the hall.
I cannot be parted
From my new football.

I kick it in the driveway.
I kick it in the street.
I dazzle all the neighbours
With my famous football feet.

I kick it in the garden
Or in the school playground
I kick it in the underpass
Anywhere around.

I kick it on the playing fields
Or in my gran's back yard
I swerve towards the lamp-posts
And shoot it really hard.

I kick it all around the house
And at the garage door
I kick it in my bedroom
And on the kitchen floor.

I kick it in the sitting room
And even in the loo!
I kick it at my aunty's
And at the chip shop too.

Someone is sure to spot me
And want me for their team
But until then, I'll kick my ball,
And dream, dream, dream . . .

Brenda Williams

Who'd Be a Football?

It's no fun being a football.
   You get kicked out,
   booted about,
   passed around,
   bounced on the ground,
   grabbed by hands,
   whacked into the stands.
And after all that, when you're feeling quite flat . . .
   you get blown up!

Michael Coleman

The World's First Football

Where did the very first football fall?
Did it land in the land of the Neanderthal?
Was it sold in a Flintstone shopping mall
Or an ancient Athenian market stall?

Where did the very first football fall?
Did Confucius bounce it off the Chinese wall?
Was it all-weather leather? Was it large or small?
Was it in a proper game or a free-for-all?

Where did the very first football fall?
Can you find it on a pyramid in hieroglyphic scrawl?
Did the Romans kick it around in Gaul
Or a Viking crew in an ancestral hall?

Where did the very first football fall?
At the little boots of Leprechauns in County Donegal
Or was it wrought in rubber by a native of Nepal
Or did they kick a coconut in sunny Senegal?

So where *did* the very first football fall?
Does anyone have any idea at all . . . ? No!

Nick Toczek

Easy Game

Swerve to left, swerve to right,
Ball at twinkling feet,
The sound of loud, adoring crowd
Is music, oh, so sweet.

Beat three slow defenders,
Shoot to goalie's right,
Arms outstretched and helpless—
What a marvellous sight.

Crowd now quite ecstatic,
Ball flies into net—
Computer soccer's easy
As you switch off TV set . . .

Clive Webster

The Goalkeeper's Dream

I'm facing an attack.
Here comes the cross.
Up go the heads
And up I fly
Above them all
To tip the ball
Round the bedpost.

John Coldwell

Fantasy Football

At night I play football in my head
under lights . . .
it's better that way—
you don't get kicked
     sent off
     or covered in mud.
Sometimes I play for United,
sometimes for my country,
but usually for a team of my own
where I am the captain
     manager
     coach
     and leading goal scorer.
I love playing football—
in my head.
     In bed.

Peter Dixon

Five-a-Side Mythical Beast Football

Centaur? You go up front. Striker.
Centaur-forward, you could say!
Just my joke.
Pegasus? Right wing.
No, you can use the left one too.
That's your position. Right wing.
All that speed. Hefty kick. Brilliant!
Unicorn? Left wing.
And this time, don't try to head it!
You've burst six balls already this season.
Minotaur? Man's body, bull's head.
You stay at the back.
But no rough stuff. Not like last week.
Should have told them not to wear red.
Dragon. In goal.
No, it's not because you're useless.
Just spread those wings. Can't go wrong.
And if the ball's going past you,
Burn it.
Now. Are you fit? Ready?
It's a tough one this week.
Back Street Primary, Year 3.
Now they're *real* beasts!

Paul Bright

My Gran—Soccer Fan

She really gets excited:
She shouts, 'Shoot!' and 'What a star!'
'Yellow card!' and 'Penalty!'
And, 'Ooh, it hit the bar!'

That's my gran, a soccer fan:
She's got a comfy chair,
And if there's football on TV
She's certain to be there.

'Fancy missing that!' she'll say
As a striker shoots just wide.
'I could have scored a goal from there.
I don't believe he tried.'

And when the goalie fumbles
She says, 'Hopeless! In a dream!
I bet I could do better
If they'd pick me for the team.'

And I get this mental picture:
Gran, like an acrobat,
Diving to save a penalty . . .

She says, 'What are you smiling at?'

Eric Finney

Strip Cartoon

My mum put my strip
In the washing machine
With a dress of deep dark red.
My strip went in white,
But now it's a sight
And I refuse to be seen.
I'd rather drop dead
Or hide in the shed
Than turn up in pink
For the team!

Brenda Williams

My Mum's Put Me on the Transfer List

On Offer:

one nippy striker, eight years old
has scored seven goals this season
has nifty footwork and a big smile
knows how to dive in the penalty box
can get filthy and muddy within two
    minutes
guaranteed to wreck his kit each week
this is a **FREE TRANSFER**
but he comes with running expenses
weeks of washing shirts and shorts
socks and vests, a pair of trainers
needs to scoff huge amounts
of chips and burgers, beans and apples
pop and cola, crisps and oranges
endless packets of chewing gum.
This offer open until the end of the
    season
I'll have him back then
at least until the cricket starts.
Any takers?

David Harmer

The Night Before the Match

The night before the match
I lie awake in bed
With thoughts of what might happen
Whirling round my head.

What if there's an open goal
And somehow I fail to score?
What if I miss a penalty
And we lose instead of draw?

What if I miss a tackle
And give a goal away?
What if I get a red card?
What will people say?

What if I'm clean through
And I slip and tread on the ball?
What if I'm ill in the morning
And can't even play at all?

The night before the match
It's always the same.
Why can't I feel like Dad who says:
'Don't worry. It's only a game.'

John Foster

Before the Game

Socks: always left first, then right, *after* saying
United, backwards, three times: 'detinu, detinu, detinu'.
Pieces of orange to be handed out then
Eaten in the changing room, just before leaving. If
Raining, Robbo first, then in numerical order: if
Sunny, Snapper first, then in reverse numerical order.
Touch toes twice, in the centre-circle, but
If we have to change ends, after the toss,
Touch toes, *outside* the centre-circle, again.
If we win the toss, *never* change ends—*ever*.
Only tuck your shirt in just before kick-off:
Never leave your shirt hanging out—*ever*.
Superstitious—who says we're superstitious?

Mike Johnson

My Dog Ate My Shin Pads

My dog ate my shin pads
and now I've none to wear.
He snuffled through my kit bag
and dragged them to his lair.

Underneath the table,
he licked them first, then sucked,
to make them nice and tender
and soften up the muck.

He chewed and gnawed and nibbled
and now my pads won't fit.
They're mangled, pulped, and soggy
and flecked with spitty bits.

My shins are bruised and battered,
but my dog doesn't care.
When he ate my shin pads
he wasn't playing fair.

Jane Clarke

White Boots

If I had white boots
Like Beckham,
Maybe then I could play.
Maybe then I wouldn't trip up
Whenever the ball came my way.
Maybe the captain would pick me,
And I'd score with my very first kick.
The whole school would cheer
As goal number two
Found the net from my overhead flick.

Never again would I sit on the ball,
Or run the wrong way up the pitch,
Or pass to their striker, or let in six goals
Or have to lie down with a stitch,
If I had white boots
Like Beckham.

Daphne Kitching

These Are the Boots

These are the boots
That kicked the ball
That scored the goal
For my team.

This is the boy
Who wore the boots
That kicked the ball
That scored the goal
For my team.

This is the cup
They gave to the boy
Who wore the boots
That kicked the ball
That scored the goal
For my team.

This is ME
Holding the cup,
For I am the boy
Who wore the boots
That kicked the ball
That scored the goal
For my team!

Cynthia Rider

Sporting Delusions

I'm a panther
I'm an acrobat
I'm an athlete so supreme
I'm a spinning ballerina
I'm a Herculean dream.

I'm a supple tightrope walker
I am loose-limbed
I'm so fit
I am bendy, bouncy, leapy
every single bit.

I also have my off days
as I stand here on the line
I'm a small and tearful goalie
and, so far, I've let in nine.

Stewart Henderson

The Dribbler

I am the dribbler
I'm loaded with skill
I go past opponents
Like they're all standing still.

I beat them with ease
And I don't like to boast
But defenders all say
It's like tackling a ghost!

I'm fresh as a daisy
A fitness fanatic
I don't have to think
It all comes automatic.

I dummy the full back
And nutmeg the sweeper
Then weave through the box
And chip over the keeper.

It's all done with balance
And football control
I squeeze on the trigger
And score a great goal!

Granville Lawson

Celebration

When I get the ball
I whizz down the wing,
Dribble it past
The opposing team,
Cross to our striker,
My best mate Joel,
And whoopee—
It's a goal.

Then . . .
Hell for leather
We race towards each other
CLASH our wheelchairs together.

Frances Nagle

Playground Ace

What a brilliant footballer!
What a playground ace!
Just watch that ball control:
What skill, what style, what pace!
As defender or as striker
This player's got the lot:
In goal, saves penalties—
Or scores them from the spot.
At free kicks and corners
This player's supreme—

I want you to meet Mary,
The captain of our team.

Eric Finney

Our Song

We are the Amazons,
We're the very best.
Queens of the football pitch,
Miles above the rest.

We can shoot, we can save,
We can control mid-field.
We are the Amazons
Who never, never yield.

Football. Football.
It's what we live for.
Ball at our feet,
Mud and sweat,
The crowd in uproar.

We are the Amazons,
We're the very best
And we wait impatiently
To face the final test:

Amazons v. Rovers
For anyone who enjoys
Witnessing a massacre
When we destroy . . . The Boys.

Frances Nagle

Talk Us Through It, Charlotte

Well I shouldn't't've been playin' really
Only there to watch me brother.
My friend fancies his friend, y'know.
Anyway they was a man short.

Stay out on the wing, they said
Give 'em something to think about.
So I did that for about an hour:
Never passed to me or anything.

The ball kind of rebounded to me.
I thought, I'll have a little run with it.
I mean, they wasn't passin' to me
Was they? So off I went.

I ran past this first boy
He sort of fell over.
It was a bit slippery on that grass
I will say that for him.

Two more of 'em come at me
Only they sort of tackled each other
Collided—arh.* I kept going.
There was this great big fat boy.

One way or another I kicked it
Through his legs and run round him.
That took a time. Me brother
Was shouting, Pass it to me, like.

Well like I said, I'd been there an hour.
They never give *me* a pass
Never even spoke to me
Or anything. So I kept going.

Beat this other boy somehow
Then there was just the goalie.
Out he came, spreadin' himself
As they say. I was really worried.

I thought he was going to hug me.
So I dipped me shoulder like they do
And the goalie moved one way, y'know
And I slammed it in the net.

Turned out afterwards it was the winner.
The manager said I was very good.
He wants me down at trainin' on Tuesday.
My friend says she's comin' as well.

Allan Ahlberg

Rhymes with 'car'—Charlotte's a Black Country girl.

When Mum Takes Me Football Training

Mum gets out her old bike and pedals like crazy
she makes me run to the park
I get red faced and breathless.
When we arrive we play one against one
she picks up the football and kicks it hard
as high as a bird in the big blue sky
it floats up there like a lost balloon,
comes thundering down and I say to myself
'Do I dare head it? Do I? Yes!'
But I don't and I miss it, nearly fall over
and head it back on the fourth bounce
better still trap it, twist past three defenders
and run like a dart for the penalty spot
draw back my foot and belt it for goal.
My mum does her arms stretched, starfish-shaped
leap-like-a-cat save, and tips it just round the post
and we sit and laugh, then buy an ice cream
take our time going home.

David Harmer

When Dad Took Me Football Training

He put on his new trainers
he put on his new jogging bottoms
he put his fancy new football
in the car with the dog.

We drove to the park
I got out and went in goal
I stood there for ages.

Dad kicked the ball
the dog brought it back
Dad sidefooted the ball
the dog pushed it back
Dad toe-poked the ball
the dog shoved it back
Dad tapped the ball
the dog rolled it back.

The sun came out. The dog rolled over.
Dad lay on the grass and went to sleep.
I booted the ball into Dad's back.

He grunted
the dog barked down his ear
so we all got into the car
and Dad drove us home.

David Harmer

Match of the Year

I am delivered to the stadium by chauffeur-driven limousine.
Gran and Grandpa give me a lift in their Mini.

I change into my sparkling clean world-famous designer strip.
*I put on my brother's shorts and the T-shirt with tomato
    ketchup stains.*

I give my lightweight professional boots a final shine.
I rub the mud off my trainers.

The coach gives me a final word of encouragement.
Dave, the sports master, tells me to get a move on.

I jog calmly through the tunnel into the stadium.
I walk nervously on to the windy sports field.

The crowd roars.
Gran and Grandpa shout, 'There's our Jimmy!'

The captain talks last-minute tactics.
'Pass to me or I'll belt you.'

The whistle goes. The well-oiled machine goes into action.
Where did the ball go?

I intercept a speeding pass and trap it neatly with my left foot.
The ball lands at my feet.

I pass it skilfully to our international star, Bernicci.
*I kick it away. Luckily, Big Bernard stops it before it goes over
the line.*

A free kick is awarded to the visiting Premier team. I'm part of
the impregnable defence.
*The bloke taking the kick looks six feet tall—and just as
wide . . .*

I stop the ball with a well-timed leap and head it expertly up the
field.
The ball thwacks me on the head.

The crowd shouts my name! 'Jim-meee! Jim-meee! Jim-meee!'
Gran says, 'Eee, our Jim's fallen over.'

I don't remember any more.

Trevor Millum

United's Red

United's red.
City's blue.
The ref needs glasses
And so do you.

Little Jack Horner

Little Jack Horner took a shot.
The goalie was unsighted.
Jack Horner scored.
The crowd all roared.
They'd beaten Man United!

Old King Cole

Old King Cole was a very fine manager,
A very fine manager was he.
He didn't believe in 4–4–2.
He always played 4–3–3.

Each of his teams had very fine strikers,
Oh, very fine strikers had he.
No team was there
That could compare
With King Cole and his strikers three.

Wee Willie Winkie

Wee Willie Winkie jumps up and down
In front of the TV in his nightgown,
Yelling with delight as the captain steps up
To score from the spot and win the World Cup.

Mary Had a Cockerel

Mary had a cockerel,
Which came from White Hart Lane
And every time that Tottenham scored
It crowed and crowed again.

Save-a-shot, Save-a-shot, Goalie Man

Save-a-shot, Save-a-shot, Goalie man
Kick it upfield as far as you can.
Dive on it. Pounce on it. Block it with your feet.
Push it round the post and keep a clean sheet.

John Foster

The Perfect Score

A nil–nil score is a ghastly bore:
I mean, why did they bother to play?
One–nil and one–one aren't really much fun
But three–two is almost OK.
Six–nil: that's a bit one-sided.
(Bet a goalkeeper gets the blame!)
Five–four? Now you're talking!
Bet that was a ding-dong game.
Yes, the perfect score has goals galore
And it happened yesterday:
Twenty-a-side on the playground—
4C versus 4A.
The game was a killer, a total thriller,
You just couldn't ask for more:
No one defended and so it all ended
In a fourteen–fourteen draw.

Eric Finney

Fair Play

Yesterday
Sam, Sarah, George, and me
beat
Nick, Kate, David, and Chris
85 to nil
in a lunchtime soccer match.
Today
Nick and Kate are playing handball,
David's in the library,
Chris is climbing the equipment
and we have
no one
to play soccer against.
It just isn't fair.

Steven Herrick

Team Talk

'My team's better than your team.
We've got the best goal-getter.'

'If you think that, you're in a dream.
I'm telling you: my team's better.'

'My team's spending millions
On a really brilliant goalie.'

'Well, my team's spending squillions
On an Italian called Ravioli.'

'We've got the best supporters
And our manager's a world-beater.'

'Your centre-forward's a tortoise.
Ours is as fast as a cheetah.'

'I think he needs specs to find the goal:
I've seen him miss from a foot.'

'Yours is hopeless at ball-control.
Does he play with both eyes shut?'

'Rubbish! He's got very tricky feet.
I've seen him get goals galore.'

'Hey, what about when our teams meet . . .'

'I think it might be a draw.'

Eric Finney

Samson United

They're the strongest team in the league—
Not because they're the best,
But because they're stuck at the bottom
And have to prop up the rest . . .

Clive Webster

Poem for the First Day of the Football Season

Brand new start,
last season is history and meaningless.

My team has no points
and neither has yours.

All things are possible
and all glory dreamable.

Everything is winnable.
Potential is unmissable.

The peak of faith is scaleable.
The mountain of hope is touchable.
The summit of belief, believable.

Ten to three on that first Saturday
and nothing dulls the taste.

Excitement and anticipation
tangible and tasteable.

Unparalleled success attainable
this could be the best season of our lives.

Paul Cookson

Poem for the Last Day of the Football Season

Dreams in tatters
Hopes in rags
Blown away
Like paper bags

Early exits
From each cup
My team down
Your team up

Shadows lengthen
The worst I fear
But I'll be back
Same time next year.

Paul Cookson

Football Magic

We've come to see a football match
My dad, my mum, and me.
We've come to see it at the ground
Instead of on TV.

We queue outside for ages
In the wind and cold and rain.
I tell my mum and dad
That I'm not coming here again.

I dream of being back at home
Curled up on our settee.
I don't know why we came now—
It's much better on TV.

You can't turn down the sound here
Or switch over when you're bored.
Or see an instant replay
Of the goal that's just been scored.

And everything looks tiny—
I will never see the ball.
I don't know why we bothered
Coming all this way at all.

But then the wind stops blowing
And the players all run out.
The ref blows on his whistle
And the crowd begins to shout.

We chant and sing and clap our hands
When our team's playing well.
And when they score a brilliant goal
We cheer and scream and yell.

Yes, when your team is winning
There's a magic that you feel.
There's nothing better in the world
Than seeing it for real.

Marcus Parry

Back Seat Manager

Why aren't they playing the new boy up front,
He cost us enough, goodness' sake,
And there he is, sat on the bench, chewing gum,
How much more can a loyal fan take?

Why don't they bring on a sub? Number ten
Is limping, I saw him back there,
Dodgy tackle, it's true, but he's barely five foot
And he can't win a ball in the air.

Why aren't we marking their men, you can see
That their goalie is falling asleep?
Come *on*, lads, wake up, only four minutes left,
I've seen livelier fields full of sheep!

Why is *he* taking the penalty? All of
His shots this last month have been wide—
It's a goal! Yes! Result! As I've said all along,
We're by far the superior side.

Petonelle Archer

Back to Basics

We can do without the 4–4–2
Forget the 4–3–3
I'd rather not play 4–2–4
Or the new shape 'Christmas tree'.

I'm through with cute formations
They're really quite a bore
Let's get back to basics, lads
Just kick the ball and score.

Richard Caley

Roboref!

It's official, pay attention!
Here's a top class league invention.
This new breed of referee
Has a microchip where his brain should be
Needs no glasses—X-ray vision
No one questions his decision.
In control—a dictator
Roboref! Terminator!

Electronic and bionic
Pre-programmed and supersonic
Nothing guessed or estimated
Every angle calculated
Perfection—guaranteed precision
Always the correct decision
On the pitch there's no one greater
Roboref! Terminator!

Computer age technology
Has built this perfect referee
Everybody toes the line
Managers don't question time
Everything is fair and clean
With this fault-free mean machine
'I'll be back!' says the man in black
'You know I'll see you later!'
No foul fools break the rules with . . .
Roboref! Terminator!

Paul Cookson

The Spectator's Lament

Have you lost your specs, Ref?
Has your whistle lost its pea?
That really was a foul, Ref
Don't say you didn't see!

Has someone slipped you a 'bung', Ref?
That clearly was off-side!
Why is it your decisions
Are always against *my* side?

John Cotton

Dick Tater

I am a little linesman.
I've got a little flag.
Oh, how I love to waggle it.
Wag, wag, wag, wag, wag, wag.

My happiest of memories
(I laughed until I cried!)
Was when that striker
Scored three times,
But I signalled him offside!

(It was curious
To see him so furious.)

John Kitching

Weak End

End of the match.
Lost. Feeling bitter.
Crowd all gone home.
Ground covered with litter.

Floodlights switched off.
Flags all lie dead.
Birds peck at worms.
Players in bed.

Sad home supporters
Unable to speak,
Dreaming, and hoping
For better next week.

John Kitching

Chippy Breath

After football
my dad buys me fish and chips
and my hot chippy breath
makes clouds in the air
and rain on the windows
of the bus
all the way home.

I write the score
on the wet glass
—but only when we win.

Michael Rosen

Football's Getting Daft

Grandad says,
Football's getting daft.
Not like when he was a lad.
Back then
It was a game of skill.
An honour
To play for your team.
And all you wanted was
To play in front of the Queen.
He says,
It's all about money these days.
Being in movies,
On television,
Marrying a pop star,
Fancy haircuts and
Fast cars.
He says,
Wish I was a football star these days.

Damian Harvey

The Price of Victory

'I've got terrible indigestion,'
The football supporter said.
'I can't go out to celebrate.
I'll have to stay in bed.'

'It serves you right!' said his wife.
'You should never have said that
If your team ever won the cup
You'd go and eat your hat!'

John Foster

That's Football!

Football thrills, magic skills
World class saves, Mexican waves
Four two four, goals galore
Celebration, relegation
Midfield runners, Magpies, Gunners
Dead ball star hits the bar
Golden boots, substitutes
Tight defence, Chairman tense
Winter freeze, referees
Strikers, sweepers, wingbacks, keepers
Free kicks, crosses, nervous bosses
Win or lose, come on, you blues
Eat it, drink it, talk it, think it
Other sports are not the same,
That's football—what a game!

Granville Lawson

Index of titles/first lines

(First lines in italic)

ACKNOWLEDGEMENTS

We are grateful for permission to reproduce the following poems:

Allan Ahlberg: 'Allan Ahlberg' from *Friendly Matches* (Viking, 2001), copyright © Allan Ahlberg 2001, reprinted by permission of Penguin Books. **Michael Coleman:** 'Who'd Be a Footballer', copyright © Michael Coleman 2002, first published in this collection by permission of Pollinger Limited on behalf of the author. **Paul Cookson:** 'Poem for the First Day of the Football Season' and 'Poem for the Last Day of the Football Season' both from *Very Best of Paul Cookson* (Macmillan, 2001), copyright © Paul Cookson 2001, reprinted by permission of the author. **Eric Finney:** 'Playground Ace' copyright © Eric Finney 2000, first published in *Sack Race – Sports and Games Poems* edited by John Foster (Oxford University Press, 2000), reprinted by permission of the author. **John Foster:** 'The Night Before the Match' from *Word Wizard* (Oxford University Press, 2001), copyright © John Foster 2001, reprinted by permission of the author. **Stewart Henderson:** 'Sporting Delusions' from the collection *Who Left Grandad at the Chipshop?* (Lion Publishing, 2001), copyright © Stewart Henderson 2001, reprinted by permission of the author. **Steven Herrick:** 'Fair Play' from *Love Poems and Leg Spinners* (University of Queensland Press, 2001), reprinted by permission of the author and publisher. **John Kitching:** 'Dick Tater', copyright © John Kitching 1998, first published in *They Think It's All Over* poems chosen by David Orme (Macmillan Children's Books, 1998), and 'Weak End', copyright © John Kitching 2000, first published in *Football Fever* edited by John Foster (Oxford University Press, 2000), both reprinted by permission of the author. **Tony Mitton:** 'Football on the Brain', copyright © Tony Mitton 1995 first published in *You'll Never Walk Alone More Football Poems* chosen by David Orme (Macmillan, 1995), reprinted by permission of the author. **Frances Nagle:** 'Celebration' from *You Can't Call a Hedgehog Hopscotch* (Dagger Press, 1999), copyright © Frances Nagle 1999, reprinted by permission of the author. **Chris Riley:** 'Backyard Kickin', copyright © Chris Riley 1995, first published in *You'll Never Walk Alone: More Football Poems* chosen by David Orme (Macmillan, 1995), reprinted by permission of the author. **Michael Rosen:** 'Chippy Breath' from *Centrally Heated Knickers* (Puffin, 2000), copyright © Michael Rosen 2000, reprinted by permission of PFD on behalf of Michael Rosen. **Nick Toczek:** 'The World's First Football' first published in a longer version in *Kick It!* (Macmillan Children's Books, 2002),copyright © Nick Toczek 2002, reprinted by permission of the author. **Bernard Young:** 'Football Fever', first published in *Brilliant* (Kingston Press, 2000), copyright © Bernard Young 2000, reprinted by permission of the author.

All other poems are published for the first time in this collection by permission of their authors:

Petonelle Archer: 'Back Seat Manager', copyright © Petonelle Archer 2002; **Ian Bland:** 'Live Football from Pete Symmonds's Garden', copyright © Ian Bland 2002; **Paul Bright:** '5-a-side Mythical Beast Football', copyright © Paul Bright 2002; **Dave Calder:** 'Wiz', copyright © Dave Calder 2002; **Richard Caley:** 'Back to Basics', copyright © Richard Caley 2002; **Jane Clarke:** 'My Dog Ate My Shin Pads' , copyright © Jane Clarke 2002; **John Coldwell:** 'The Goalkeeper's Dream', copyright © John Coldwell 2002; **Paul Cookson:** 'Roboref', copyright © Paul Cookson 2002; **John Cotton:** 'The Spectator's Lament' copyright © John Cotton 2002; **Peter Dixon:** 'Fantasy Football', copyright © Peter Dixon 2002; **Eric Finney:** 'My Gran – Soccer Fan', 'The Perfect Score', and 'Team Talk', all copyright © Eric Finney 2002; **John Foster:** 'Kicking In', 'Please, Mr Black', 'The Price of Victory', and 'Nonsense Football Rhymes', all copyright John Foster 2002; **David Harmer:** 'My Mum Put Me On The Transfer List', 'When Mum Takes Me Football Training', and 'When Dad Took Me Football Training', all copyright © David Harmer 2002; **Damian Harvey:** 'Football's Getting Daft', copyright © Damian Harvey 2002; **Mike Johnson:** 'Before the Game', copyright © Mike Johnson 2002; **Daphne Kitching:** 'Footballitis' and 'White Boots', both copyright © Daphne Kitching 2002; **Granville Lawson:** 'That's Football' and 'The Dribbler', both copyright © Granville Lawson 2002; **Trevor Millum:** 'Match of the Year', copyright © Trevor Millum 2002; **Frances Nagle:** 'Our Song', copyright © Frances Nagle 2002; **Marcus Parry:** 'Football Magic', copyright © Marcus Parry 2002; **Cynthia Rider:** 'These Boots', copyright © Cynthia Rider 2002; **Clive Webster:** 'Easy Game' and 'Samson United', both copyright © Clive Webster 2002; **Brenda Williams:** 'My New Football' and 'Strip Cartoon', both copyright © Brenda Williams 2002.